For everyone who dreams of freedom
—T.N.T.

For Trudy and Julia
—L.F.

Stacey Abrams and the Fight to Vote
Text copyright © 2022 by Traci N. Todd
Illustrations copyright © 2022 by Laura Freeman
Fact-checking by Esther Gim
All rights reserved. Manufactured in Italy.
No part of this book may be used or reproduced in any manner whatsoever without
written permission except in the case of brief quotations embodied in critical
articles and reviews. For information address HarperCollins Children's Books,
a division of HarperCollins Publishers, 195 Broadway, New York, NY 10007.
www.harpercollinschildrens.com
Library of Congress Control Number: 2021946934
ISBN 978-0-06-313977-0

The artist used Photoshop to create the digital illustrations for this book.
Typography by Rachel Zegar
22  23  24  25  26   RTLO   10  9  8  7  6  5  4  3  2  1
❖
First Edition

# STACEY ABRAMS
## AND THE FIGHT TO VOTE

Traci N. Todd

Illustrated by Laura Freeman

HARPER

*An Imprint of HarperCollinsPublishers*

In that faraway place where the ancestors sit, Fannie Lou heard something on the wind.

*Georgia citizens tried to exercise their constitutional rights and were still denied . . .*
*Our fight to count every vote is not about me.*
*It is about us.*

Fannie Lou called her friend Septima, who knew many things.
"Look there," Fannie Lou said. "Who is that? Talking about votes and rights denied."
Septima looked.
"Oh yes." She smiled. "That's Stacey Abrams having her say. She is one of us. Why don't you call Ida and Sojourner. They'll want to hear this story, too."

"It starts in Hattiesburg, Mississippi, where Stacey's parents—
Carolyn and Robert—fell in love. But they almost didn't meet.

"Growing up, Carolyn didn't have much. There was hardly money for
food, let alone the bus to take Carolyn to school. And of course, Jim Crow
made a hard life even harder."

"Those horrible laws," said Ida. "Seems like they should have a tougher name than Jim Crow for all the harm and hurt they caused."

The other women nodded.

"Carolyn dropped out of school for a little while," Septima continued, "but she found a way back and graduated top of her high school class. That's where she met Robert."

"Now, school was not easy for Robert.
Reading was hard. But he knew the strength
of his own mind and imagined big things."

"Carolyn and Robert married and had six children. Stacey was number two. Life wasn't easy, but the children looked after each other. Taking care of others became a family rule.

"Robert and Carolyn taught their children that one of the best ways to take care of their community is to vote. To elect people and make choices that would make the community stronger. It was a right they had both fought for, and every election day, they took their children to the polling place, closed the curtain, and imagined something more."

"Stacey had a head for imagining, too, thanks to all those books she read. Mythology, classics, a whole set of encyclopedias. And since Carolyn was a librarian, Stacey never ran out of things to read!

"Now, one of the gifts of reading is learning big, juicy words. Like *brilliant* instead of *smart*. *Complicated* instead of *hard*. *Apprehensive* instead of *afraid*. Words that can give shape to your wildest imaginings. And the only way to make those words your own is to use them. And Stacey did. *Abundantly.*"

"One day, a teacher told Stacey to keep her big words to herself.

"And do you know what Stacey did? She kept *all* of her words. Didn't say a thing. Not even when the teacher called her name. The teacher didn't like that one bit. She asked Carolyn and Robert to do something about it. They did something all right. They told that teacher to do her job and stop trying to silence their child.

"This wasn't the first time someone saw Stacey as less than she was, and it wouldn't be the last. Each time took a little bit of Stacey's spirit, but she still imagined more."

"Imagining carried Stacey to New York, to a summer camp for children who also liked big, juicy words. But they had read books she didn't know. They were published poets, concert musicians, and the children of powerful people. Suddenly Stacey didn't think she was special enough to be at the camp. By the end of the week, she was ready to go home.

"But Carolyn and Robert told her to stay right where she was. Reminded her that she was brilliant and that sometimes she would light the way. And sometimes her way would be lit by others."

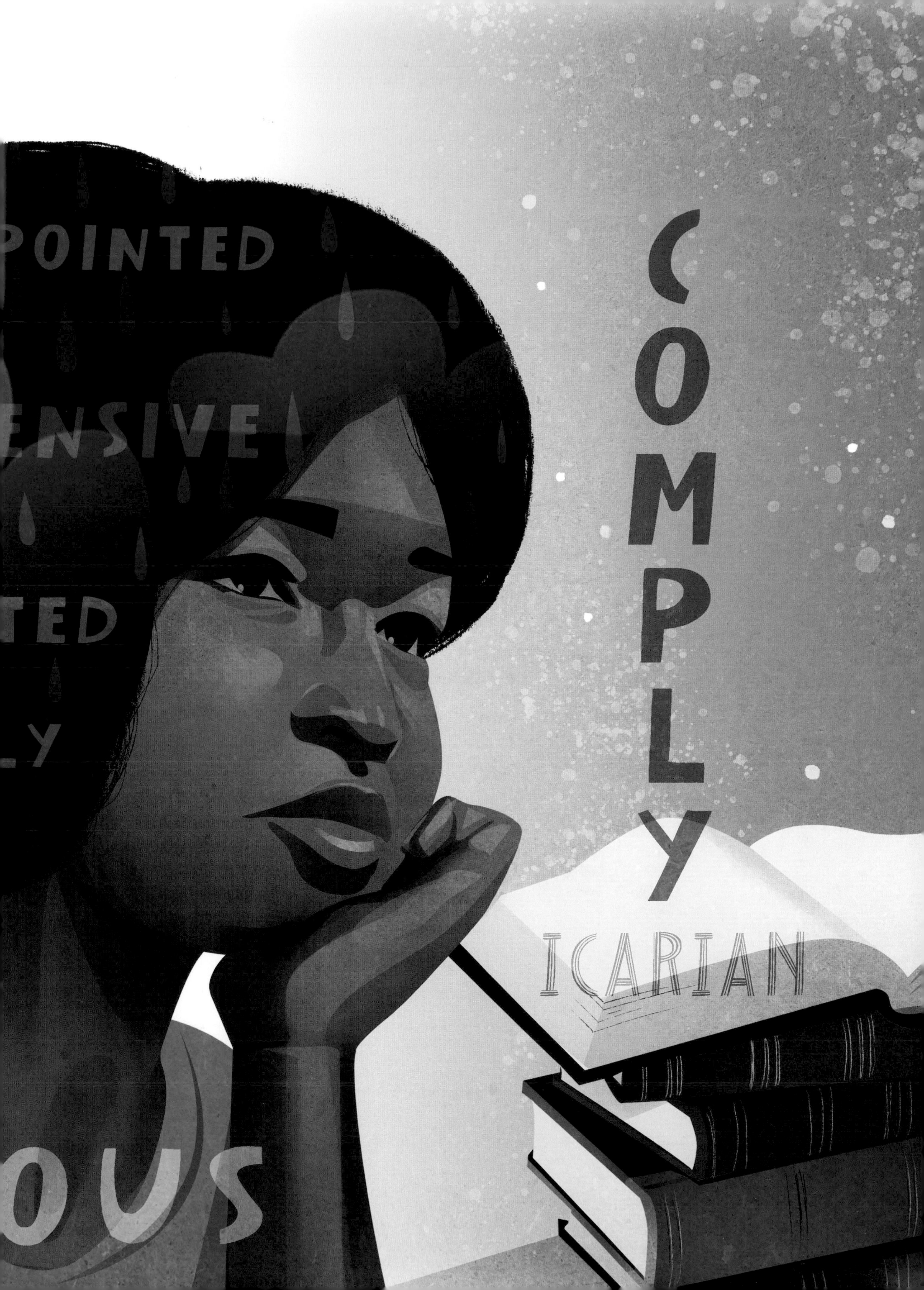
POINTED
ENSIVE
TED
LY
OUS
COMPLY
ICARIAN

"The next time Stacey saw the light was at Spelman College, in Atlanta, Georgia. Now, the right school can really shape a person, and Spelman was the right school for Stacey. She found space to protest, organize, question, and discover. She met influential people, like the college president, who nurtured her ambitions. And the mayor, who offered her a job.

"Stacey wondered what being mayor would be like. She added it to her list of things to accomplish. It was not a short list."

"And did she become mayor?" Fannie Lou asked.

"No," Septima replied. "She decided to run for governor instead."

"Not everyone thought running for governor was a good idea. Even her friends said Georgia wasn't ready.

"But Stacey imagined more. She found every corner of that state. Listened to what people had to say. Helped thousands register to vote. And, at last, it seemed she might become the first Black woman ever elected governor in the United States."

"The first . . . *ever*?" Ida said. "What year are we talking about?"

"This was 2018 . . ." Septima replied.

"Guess I shouldn't be surprised we had to wait this long . . ."

"We're still waiting, Ida. Stacey didn't win . . ."

"What happened?"

"You know that each state keeps a list of the people who can vote," Septima replied.
"Well, somehow, hundreds of thousands of names disappeared from Georgia's list.
And there weren't enough places to vote.
The few places they had were hard to get to.
And the lines were too long.
And the voting machines didn't work . . .
And you know who was in charge of this mess?
The man who won the election."

Sojourner shook her head.
"The people who couldn't vote—did they look like you and me?" she asked.
"Many of them, yes," said Septima.
Sojourner closed her eyes.
"We fought so hard," she said.

"I remember . . .

"In my day, people went on about how mighty the Constitution was, but how mighty could it be if it didn't include me? *Where are the rights for women?* I wondered. *I am as smart, strong, and hardworking as any man. I am a woman's rights!*

"I swore I would not die till all of us—Black women, too—got the right to vote. But folks took too long to do the right thing, and God had other plans."

"I remember . . ." said Ida. "I fought for our rights with white women who called me sister, then pushed me aside when they thought the South was watching. The South was so afraid of what we might do with a bit of power and imagination."

"In the end, we won the right to vote on paper, but those Southern mayors and governors did everything they could to keep it from being true."

"They surely did," said Fannie Lou. "With poll taxes, reading tests, and much, *much* worse. I remember. I once took folks to register to vote in an old school bus. The police stopped us because they said the bus was too yellow!

"I lost my job that time. Almost lost my life the next.

"We went through so much pain before anyone paid attention."

"So much," Septima agreed. "I remember. I spent a summer in Georgia once. Stood on the steps of that Albany courthouse for ten days straight, helping Black people register to vote. Guards tried to turn them away, but I said, *No. This is your right.* And in 1965, after the president finally signed that voting rights act, I went to Selma, Alabama, and taught hundreds how to sign their names."

"We fought so hard." Sojourner sighed.

The ancestors were quiet.

The wind was not.

*. . . The antidote to injustice is progress. . . . We may not share the same faith, but we are knitted together by our belief in our potential for more.*

"But see?" Septima said. "There is always hope. *That's* what's happening tonight in Georgia, Fannie Lou. Stacey is rejecting this election, calling all that nonsense what it is: a great silencing. More sneaky than in our times, but just as mighty."

"And Stacey imagines a movement. A crusade to protect the least powerful, to register everyone who is eligible to vote, and to make voting fair and easy. She will demand better for Georgia and every other state in this nation.

"And she won't do it alone."

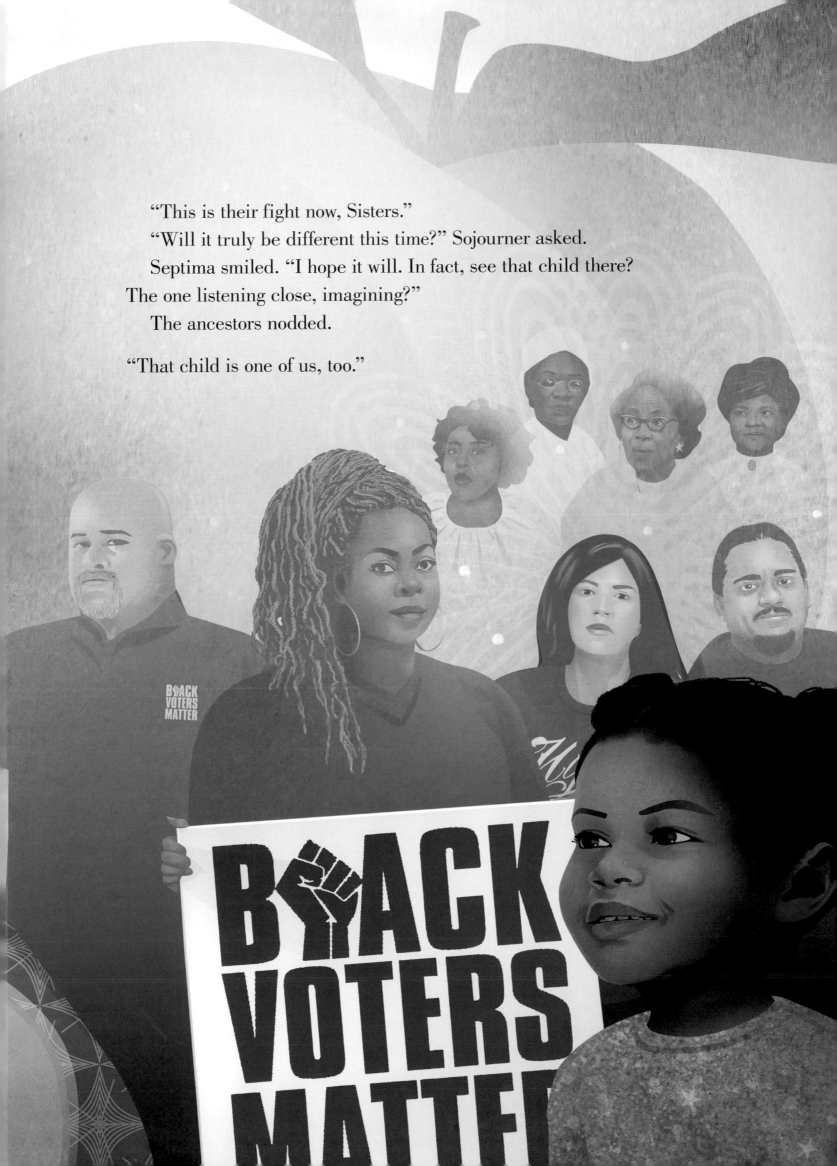

"This is their fight now, Sisters."

"Will it truly be different this time?" Sojourner asked.

Septima smiled. "I hope it will. In fact, see that child there? The one listening close, imagining?"

The ancestors nodded.

"That child is one of us, too."

## Author's Note

**W**hy did I choose to tell Stacey Abrams's story through the imagined voices of Septima Poinsette Clark, Sojourner Truth, Ida B. Wells, and Fannie Lou Hamer? Because in countless ways, Stacey is continuing the work these—and many other—women started. Like Stacey, they knew how powerful and essential the right to vote is and saw how easily it could be denied.

One additional note: If Stacey Abrams had won in 2018, she would have been the first Black woman *elected* governor. But in 1972, State Senator Barbara Jordan served as governor of Texas for one day, when both the governor and lieutenant governor were out of state. Barbara went on to represent Texas in the U.S. House of Representatives.

## Who Is Stacey Abrams?

**Born: Madison, Wisconsin, 1973**

Stacey Abrams is a politician, activist, entrepreneur, and successful novelist. Her parents, Carolyn and Robert, raised Stacey and her five siblings with three guiding ideas: go to church, go to school, and be of service. Being of service meant anything from taking care of the family to taking care of the larger community.

To those three ideas, Stacey added another: work hard to become more. Growing up in Gulfport, Mississippi, Stacey didn't always have running water, but she always had books. The worlds she discovered helped her see what was possible, even as teachers and others who were supposed to support her doubted her potential.

Stacey went to Spelman College in Atlanta, Georgia, founded in 1881 to empower Black women freed from enslavement. Over one hundred years later, when Stacey arrived, she could feel that Spelman expected its students to "dream beyond our narrow understanding of what we could be." Neighboring Spelman was Morehouse, a school for men; Clark Atlanta University; and Morehouse School of Medicine. Together, this group of historically Black colleges was known as the Atlanta University Center, or AUC.

At Spelman, Stacey became an activist. In 1991, a Black man in Los Angeles named Rodney King was beaten by four police officers. The beating was recorded on camera for all to see. A year later, when a court decided the police officers were not guilty of doing anything wrong, Black communities all over the United States—including Atlanta—erupted. As the protests wore on, the Atlanta police swarmed the AUC and threw tear gas as if the campuses were a threat. The news reported stories about what was happening that were untrue. What could Stacey do to be of service? She organized as many students as she could to call the news stations and demand that they do better. Whenever someone asked who was calling, the students said, "Stacey Abrams."

One news station invited Stacey to attend a televised meeting with the mayor of Atlanta. When she told *him* to do better, he hired her to work as a research assistant.

Throughout college, Stacey kept and updated a spreadsheet of her goals and how to achieve them. On the list was to become mayor of Atlanta, but, in time, Stacey realized she wanted more. She wanted to be governor of the state of Georgia. In 2010, she cofounded an organization that created jobs and helped support small Georgia businesses. Another organization she founded, the New Georgia Project, helped register more than two hundred thousand voters from 2014 to 2016. She was ready to run.

In May 2018, Stacey won the Democratic primary, which meant the people had chosen her to represent them against Republican candidate Brian Kemp in the race for governor. Kemp was Georgia's secretary of state. Among other things, he was in charge of the voter registration process and how elections work. While Stacey worked to register voters between 2012 and 2018, Kemp's office *un*registered over one million. Most of these voters were people of color.

In November 2018, when Kemp received more votes than Stacey and she knew she wasn't going to win, this is what she had to say:

*I acknowledge that former secretary of state Brian Kemp will be certified as the victor in the 2018 gubernatorial election.*

*But to watch an elected official—who claims to represent the people of this state—baldly pin his hopes for election on the suppression of the people's democratic right to vote has been truly appalling. So, to be clear, this is not a speech of concession.*

To some experts, the way people were kept from voting in Georgia in 2018 felt similar to the very things Fannie Lou Hamer and Septima Poinsette Clark had fought against not so long ago.

Together with organizations like Black Voters Matter, Mijente, and ProGeorgia, Stacey's New Georgia Project registered hundreds of thousands of voters across Georgia, changing the outcome of the 2020 presidential election.

Stacey will run for governor again in 2022. She is always imagining more.

# Who Was Sojourner Truth?

**Born: Rifton, New York, 1797–1883**

Sojourner Truth was known as much for her physical presence as for the power of her words. Born enslaved, she believed she could talk to God, and when He told her to walk to freedom, she listened. As a free woman, she knew her purpose in life was to travel and teach, so she changed her name from Isabella to Sojourner Truth (to sojourn means to travel). Sojourner spoke out against the enslavement of Black people and for the rights of women. At an 1851 women's rights convention in Akron, Ohio, Sojourner delivered a now-famous speech in which she said:

> *I am a woman's rights.*
> *I have as much muscle as any man and can do as much work as any man. . . .*
> *You need not be afraid to give us our rights for fear we will take too much, for we can't take more than our pint'll hold.*

This version of the speech does not include the famous line "Ain't I a woman?" because scholars debate whether Sojourner Truth actually said it. The above is the only version of her speech Sojourner herself approved.

# Who Was Ida B. Wells?

**Born: Holly Springs, Mississippi, 1862–1931**

Ida B. Wells was an activist and newspaper journalist. As a journalist, she wrote the truth about why mobs of white people were lynching (killing) Black people in the South. White people claimed they were protecting themselves. But Ida uncovered the truth: white people were killing Black people because Black people were making money and gaining power. When Ida published her findings, white people threatened to lynch her, too.

Ida fled the South, settling in Chicago, Illinois. There she cofounded the Alpha Suffrage Club (ASC), which fought for Black women's right to vote. When we think about the women's suffrage (the right to vote) movement, led by people like Elizabeth Cady Stanton and Susan B. Anthony, we often think the fight was for all women. But Black women and other women of color were often left out of that fight. In 1913, Stanton and Anthony's National American Woman Suffrage Association (NAWSA) invited Ida and the ASC to join their 1913 protest parade in Washington, DC. When Ida arrived, she was told that she and the ASC had to march at the back. Why? The NAWSA wanted an amendment (change) to the U.S. Constitution granting women the right to vote, but they needed the support of the South. Southerners already made it nearly impossible for Black men to vote, and they certainly did not want Black women to have that power. So the NAWSA didn't want to seem too friendly toward Ida and the ASC. But Ida ignored their request and marched at the front of the parade.

# Who Was Septima Poinsette Clark?

**Born: Charleston, South Carolina, 1898–1987**

Septima Poinsette Clark was a teacher who encouraged her students to read everything—from catalogs to dry-cleaning bags—to gain a better understanding of the world. She joined the National Association for the Advancement of Colored People (NAACP), cofounded in 1909 by Ida B. Wells, and developed educational courses for citizenship workshops and a training program for civil rights leaders. Rosa Parks attended one of her workshops shortly before she refused to give up her seat on a Montgomery, Alabama, bus.

These workshops evolved to help Black Southerners learn what they needed to pass the literacy tests required to register to vote. By giving Black people what they needed to overcome this hurdle, Septima helped thousands of Black people add their names to the voter rolls.

# Who Was Fannie Lou Hamer?

**Born: Montgomery County, Mississippi, 1917–1977**

Fannie Lou Hamer was in her forties before she realized Black people had the right to vote. When she heard members of the Student Nonviolent Coordinating Committee (SNCC) talk about registering to vote, she was inspired to register herself. (SNCC, pronounced "snick," was a student protest group organized, in part, by Ella Baker and Dr. Martin Luther King Jr.)

In August 1962, Fannie and seventeen others took an old school bus to a voter registration site. Unfortunately, she failed the unfair literacy test required to register. On the way home, police officers arrested and fined the bus driver because, they said, the bus was "too yellow." That night, Fannie Lou's boss fired her for attempting to register and forced her out of her home.

The next year, Fannie Lou attended a citizenship class taught by Septima Poinsette Clark. On the way back from the class, Fannie Lou was arrested and taken to jail, where police beat her and forced other inmates to do the same. She was nearly killed.

But still Fannie Lou didn't give up. In 1964, she helped organize Freedom Summer, which brought people from all over the country to help register Black voters in Mississippi and throughout the South. She was a founder of the Mississippi Freedom Democratic Party and demanded to participate in the Democratic National Convention of 1964.

# Voting Rights in the United States: A Timeline

**1776:** The Declaration of Independence includes the words:

*We hold these truths to be self-evident, that all men are created equal, that they are endowed by their creator with certain unalienable Rights. . . . That to secure these rights, Governments are instituted among Men, deriving their just powers from the consent of the governed.*

In other words, in this new government, American citizens would choose who was in charge of running the country. In the beginning, the right to vote was only granted to white Protestant men twenty-one or older who owned land. (They claimed to "own" the land, but in truth, it was taken from the Indigenous people already living there.) The one exception was New Jersey. The New Jersey state constitution said anyone who owned a certain amount of land could vote—including women.

**1776:** Pennsylvania is the first state to say that landownership isn't required to vote. Now all white men in the state can vote. (In 1856, North Carolina becomes the last state to get rid of the land requirement.)

**1788:** The United States Constitution is ratified. It leaves it up to the states to decide who can vote, how, and when.

**1789:** George Washington is elected first president of the United States. Only about 6 percent of Americans can vote.

**1790:** The Naturalization Act is passed. It says that only "free white" immigrants can become citizens of the United States. Citizenship is required to vote.

**1807:** New Jersey bans women and Black people from voting, deciding that only tax-paying white men can vote.

**1848:** At a women's rights convention in Seneca Falls, New York, Frederick Douglass, a newspaper editor who was born into enslavement, gives a speech calling for voting rights for all, including women and Black people. The same year, after invading and colonizing Mexican land, the United States grants U.S. citizenship to people living there. But these new citizens are met with violence when they try to vote. (This land becomes New Mexico, Utah, Nevada, Arizona, California, Texas, and part of Colorado.)

**1861–65:** Thirteen states—South Carolina, Mississippi, Florida, Alabama, Georgia, Louisiana, Texas, Virginia, Arkansas, North Carolina, Tennessee, Missouri, and Kentucky—decide they do not want the federal government to interfere with their desire to enslave Black people. They denounce the U.S. government and form their own nation: the Confederate States of America. On April 12, 1861, they attack the United States and the Civil War begins. After four long years, the Confederate states surrender.

**1865:** The Thirteenth Amendment to the U.S. Constitution is ratified. It abolishes enslavement except as punishment for a crime.

**1867:** The Military Reconstruction Act outlines the terms by which the Confederate states can rejoin the union. Each state must write a new constitution and ratify the Thirteenth and Fourteenth Amendments to the U.S. Constitution. Federal troops are stationed in the states to protect the rights of formerly enslaved people.

**1868:** The Fourteenth Amendment to the U.S. Constitution is ratified. It says that formerly enslaved people are now citizens of the United States. Indigenous people living on reservations are excluded from citizenship.

**1870:** The Fifteenth Amendment to the Constitution says that men cannot be denied the right to vote because of their race. Neither women nor Indigenous people are allowed to vote. For a while, Black men—but not women—are able to vote freely, even in the former Confederacy.

**1872:** By this time in the South, more Black people have served as elected officials at the state and federal levels than ever before or after. But the Ku Klux Klan and other terrorist groups threaten the lives of Black voters and officials, and voting among Black men falls significantly.

**1877:** The election of President Rutherford B. Hayes results in the removal of federal troops from Southern states, thus ending protection for Black people. The Ku Klux Klan flourishes, and much of the social, economic, and political progress Black people had made in the South ends. This is the start of the Jim Crow era, a series of laws and measures meant to separate, dehumanize, and diminish Black people. The Jim Crow era lasts for almost one hundred years.

**1882:** The Chinese Exclusion Act says that people of Chinese ancestry cannot become U.S. citizens and therefore cannot vote.

**1884:** In *Elk v. Wilkins*, the U.S. Supreme Court decides that Indigenous people—who lived on this land long before the United States was the United States—are not citizens and therefore cannot vote.

**1880s–'90s:** The rise of poll taxes and literacy tests in the South continues to make voting difficult for Black men. White men are affected by these measures, too, but most Southern states enact "grandfather clauses," which say that if you had the right to vote before 1867, you can still vote, even if you can't pay the poll taxes or pass the literacy tests. Because Black people couldn't vote before 1867, they are excluded from grandfather clauses.

**1890:** The Indian Naturalization Act is passed, allowing all Indigenous people to apply for U.S. citizenship. Many are not interested. The U.S. government declares that Indigenous people can become American citizens if they give up their tribal connections (Dawes Act), apply for citizenship, and serve in the military.

**1920:** The Nineteenth Amendment to the Constitution grants women the right to vote, but voter intimidation is still a problem in the South.

**1922:** The Supreme Court decides that people of Japanese descent cannot become American citizens and therefore can't vote. In 1923, the court decides that people of Indian descent can't become citizens either.

**1924:** The Indian Citizenship Act declares that all Indigenous people born in the United States are citizens, but leaves the states to decide whether they can vote.

**1940:** Only about 3 percent of eligible Black men are registered to vote in the South.

**1948:** Miguel Trujillo Sr., an Isleta Pueblo man and World War II vet, sues New Mexico for the right to vote and wins. Now Indigenous people can vote in all fifty states. In 1958, North Dakota becomes the last state to grant voting rights to people living on reservations.

**1964:** The Twenty-Fourth Amendment to the Constitution eliminates poll taxes.

**1965:** In March, Dr. Martin Luther King Jr. leads thousands on a five-day, fifty-four-mile march from Selma, Alabama, to the state capitol in Montgomery, drawing national attention to the harassment and threats Black people in the South still face when they try to register to vote. In August, President Lyndon B. Johnson signs the Voting Rights Act of 1965, which abolishes literacy tests and gives the federal government the authority to take over voter registration if Black voters continue to be harassed.

**1975:** The Voting Rights Act is amended to require that voting materials are in languages other than English.

**1984:** Federal law requires that polling places be made accessible to disabled voters.

**2013:** The U.S. Supreme Court removes some of the key protections of the Voting Rights Act. As a result, several states, including Texas, Mississippi, North Carolina, South Dakota, Iowa, and Indiana, pass restrictions on voting that have the greatest impact on voters of color.

**2014:** Several organizations—including the Mexican American Legal Defense and Education Fund—work to combat the voter suppression brought about by the Supreme Court decision.

**2021:** Legislation to protect the right to vote passes the U.S. House of Representatives, including the John Lewis Voting Rights Advancement Act. Named for Georgia representative and civil rights activist John Lewis, if it passes the Senate and becomes law, the act would reinstate the protections removed in 2013 from the Voting Rights Act of 1965.

# Bibliography

### Books

Abrams, Stacey. *Lead from the Outside: How to Build Your Future and Make Real Change.* New York: Picador, 2019.

Abrams, Stacey. *Our Time Is Now.* New York: Henry Holt, 2020.

Bennett, Lerone, Jr. *Before the Mayflower: A History of Black America.* New York: Penguin, 1988.

Downs, Jim, ed. *Voter Suppression in U.S. Elections.* Athens: University of Georgia Press, 2020.

Giddings, Paula. *When and Where I Enter: The Impact of Black Women on Race and Sex in America.* New York: Morrow, 1984.

Weatherford, Carole Boston. *Voice of Freedom: Fannie Lou Hamer: Spirit of the Civil Rights Movement.* Somerville, MA: Candlewick, 2018.

### Magazine Articles

Hall, Jacquelyn Dowd, Eugene P. Walker, Katherine Mellen Charron, and David P. Cline. "Septima Clark and Women in the Civil Rights Movement." *Southern Cultures*, Summer 2010. www.southerncultures.org/article/i-train-the-people-to-do-their-own-talking-septima-clark-and-women-in-the-civil-rights-movement.

Powell, Kevin. "The Power of Stacey Abrams." *Washington Post Magazine*, May 14, 2020.

Stuart, Tessa. "Stacey Abrams Is Building a New Kind of Political Machine in the Deep South." *Rolling Stone*, March 1, 2020. www.rollingstone.com/politics/politics-features/stacey-abrams-census-voting-rights-vice-president-953173.

Timmons, Heather. "Stacey Abrams' Concession Speech Is a Powerful Critique of US Civil Rights." *Quartz*, November 19, 2018. www.qz.com/1468560/read-stacey-abrams-full-concession-speech.

### Websites

Campbell, Matthew L., and Jacqueline De León. "A History of Native Voting Rights." Native American Voting Rights Coalition. Accessed February 21, 2021. www.narf.org/cases/voting-rights.

Michals, Debra, ed. "Fannie Lou Hamer." National Women's History Museum, 2017. Accessed February 12, 2021. www.womenshistory.org/education-resources/biographies/fannie-lou-hamer.

Podell, Leslie. "The Sojourner Truth Project." Accessed February 12, 2021. www.thesojournertruthproject.com.

SNCC Digital Gateway. "Septima Clark." SNCC Legacy Project and Duke University. Accessed February 12, 2021. www.snccdigital.org/people/septima-clark.

Walker, Eugene. Interview with Septima Poinsette Clark, July 30, 1976. Southern Oral History Program Collection, University of North Carolina at Chapel Hill. Accessed February 12, 2021. https://docsouth.unc.edu/sohp/html_use/G-0017.html.